First Drawings

Dinosaurs

BIG BUDDY
FIRST DRAWINGS
BOOKS

Big Buddy Books
An Imprint of Abdo Publishing
abdopublishing.com

By Katie Lajiness

abdopublishing.com

Published by Abdo Publishing, a division of ABDO, PO Box 398166, Minneapolis, Minnesota 55439.
Copyright © 2017 by Abdo Consulting Group, Inc. International copyrights reserved in all countries. No part
of this book may be reproduced in any form without written permission from the publisher. Big Buddy Books™
is a trademark and logo of Abdo Publishing.

Printed in the United States of America, North Mankato, Minnesota.
092016
012017

Illustrations: Michael Jacobsen/Spectrum Studio
Interior Photos: Deposit Photos

Coordinating Series Editor: Tamara L. Britton
Graphic Design: Taylor Higgins, Maria Hosley

Publisher's Cataloging-in-Publication Data

Names: Lajiness, Katie, author.
Title: Dinosaurs / by Katie Lajiness.
Description: Minneapolis, MN : Abdo Publishing, 2017. | Series: First drawings |
      Includes index.
Identifiers: LCCN 2016945191 | ISBN 9781680785227 (lib. bdg.) |
      ISBN 9781680798821 (ebook)
Subjects: LCSH: Dinosaurs in art--Juvenile literature. | Drawing--Technique--
      Juvenile literature.
Classification: DDC 743.6--dc23
LC record available at http://lccn.loc.gov/2016945191

Table of Contents

Getting Started

Today, you're going to draw dinosaurs. Not sure you know how to draw? Dinosaurs are easy to **sketch** if you break them down into circles, ovals, rectangles, squares, and triangles.

To begin, you'll need paper, a sharpened pencil, a big eraser, and a flat surface. Draw each shape lightly. When these **guidelines** are light, it is easy to erase and try again.

BASIC SHAPES Circle Oval Rectangle Square Triangle

Stegosaurus

Brontosaurus

T. rex

Deinonychus

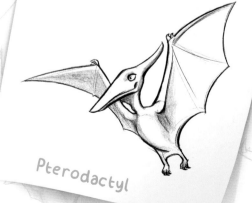

Pterodactyl

Adding Color

Once you learn to draw an object, you may want to add color. Let's learn how to mix colors and add shading.

Shading

MARKERS
Use similar colors to create shading.

PENCILS AND CRAYONS
Use less pressure for lighter shades and more pressure for darker shades.

PAINTS
Add white to lighten and black or blue to darken shades.

There are three primary colors. They are red, yellow, and blue. These colors cannot be made by mixing other colors. However, you can make many colors by mixing primary colors together.

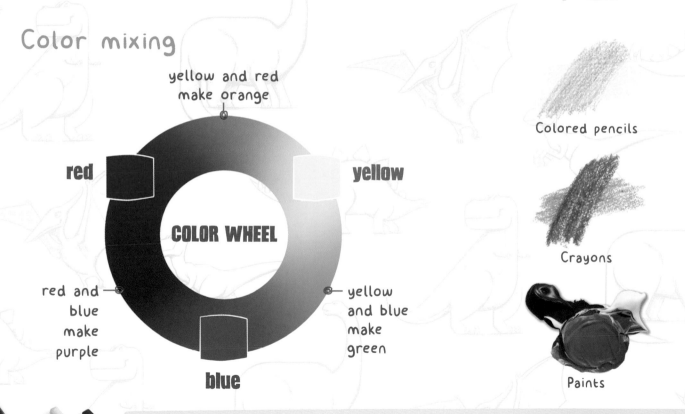

Color mixing

yellow and red make orange

red

COLOR WHEEL

yellow

red and blue make purple

yellow and blue make green

blue

Colored pencils

Crayons

Paints

Tip Create **contrast** by using colors from opposite ends of the color wheel.

Stegosaurus

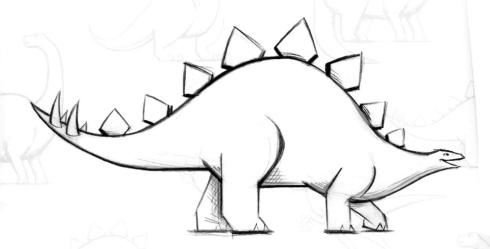

Let's learn to draw a stegosaurus!

STEP 1

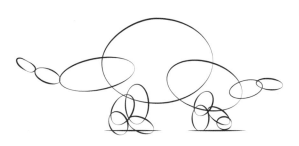

Draw basic oval **guidelines** for the head, neck, body, tail, legs, and feet.

Erase guidelines once you have the parts drawn.

STEP 2

Connect the shapes to form the dinosaur's **outline**.

STEP 3

Sketch body features such as an eye, mouth, hip, and shoulder.

STEP 4

Add triangle shapes for the plates and spikes along the dinosaur's back and tail. Draw **details** for the feet.

STEP 5

Create **texture** and shape by adding shading to your stegosaurus.

STEP 6

It's time for some color! You can add your own color and shading to personalize your drawing.

YOU DID IT!

Bravo! You drew a stegosaurus.

Brontosaurus

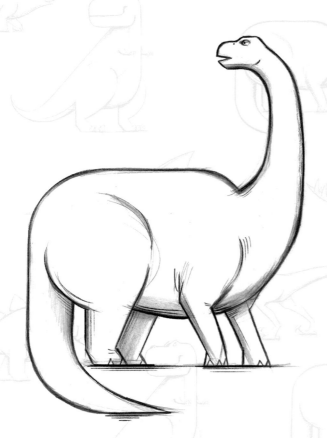

Let's learn to draw a brontosaurus!

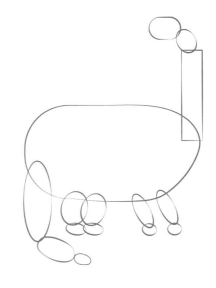

STEP 1

Draw basic oval and rectangle **guidelines** for the head, neck, body, tail, legs, and feet.

Erase guidelines once you have the parts drawn.

STEP 2

Connect the shapes to form the dinosaur's **outline**.

STEP 3

Sketch body features such as a shoulder and hip.

STEP 4

Now draw an eye and a mouth.
Add **details** to the feet.

STEP 5

Create **depth** and shape by adding
shading to your brontosaurus.

It's time for some color! You can add your own color and shading to personalize your drawing.

YOU DID IT!

Well done! You drew a brontosaurus.

15

Tyrannosaurus Rex

Let's learn to draw a *T. rex*!

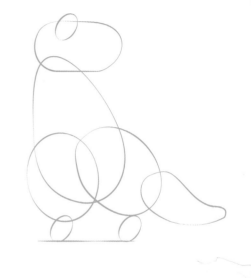

Draw basic oval **guidelines** for the head, body, tail, legs, and feet.

16

Erase guidelines once you have the parts drawn.

Connect the shapes to form the *T. rex*'s **outline**.

Sketch the dinosaur's eyes, nostrils, and mouth.

STEP 4

Fill in features such as arms and claws.

STEP 5

Create **texture** and shape by adding shading to your *T. rex*.

It's time for some color! You can add your own color and shading to personalize your drawing.

YOU DID IT!

Congratulations! You drew a *T. rex*.

Pterodactyl

Let's learn to draw a pterodactyl!

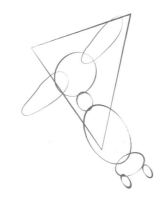

STEP 1

Draw basic oval and triangle **guidelines** for the head, body, arms, and legs.

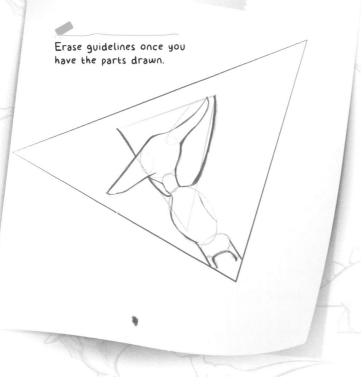

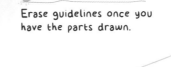

Erase guidelines once you
have the parts drawn.

STEP 2

Connect the shapes to form the pterodactyl's head and body **outline**. **Sketch** a large triangle as a **guideline** for the wings.

STEP 3

Draw the wing shape. Add the mouth and an eye.

21

STEP 4

Fill in the hands, feet, and add wing **details**.

STEP 5

Create **texture** and shape by adding shading.

It's time for some color! You can add your own color and shading to personalize your drawing.

YOU DID IT!

Yippee! You drew a pterodactyl.

Deinonychus

Let's learn to draw a deinonychus!

Draw basic oval **guidelines** for the head, neck, body, and tail.

Erase guidelines once you
have the parts drawn.

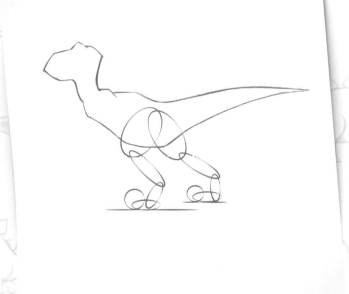

STEP 2

Connect the shapes to form the
dinosaur's **outline**.

STEP 3

Add ovals as **guidelines** for the legs
and feet.

Erase guidelines once you
have the parts drawn.

Draw the legs and clawed feet.

Sketch more oval **guidelines** for
the arm and claws.

Erase guidelines once you have the parts drawn.

STEP 6

Add the front arm with curved, clawed fingers.

STEP 7

Draw the dinosaur's right arm.

STEP 8

Sketch the dinosaur's mouth and eyes.

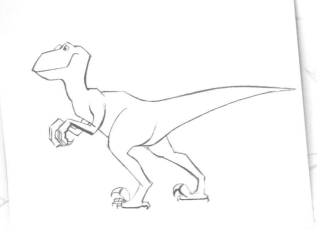

STEP 9

Create **texture** and shape by adding shading to your deinonychus.

Tools There are many tools you can use to add color such as crayons, colored pencils, paints, or markers.

It's time for some color! You can add your own color and shading to personalize your drawing.

YOU DID IT!

Yay! You drew a deinonychus.

On Your Own

To build your drawing skills, practice finding basic shapes in everyday objects. Finding basic shapes can help you draw almost anything. Use what you've learned to draw other dinosaurs. The more you draw, the better you will be!

Glossary

contrast the amount of difference in color or brightness.

depth measurement from top to bottom or from front to back.

detail a minor decoration, such as a cat's whiskers.

guideline a rule or instruction that shows or tells how something should be done.

outline the outer edges of a shape.

sketch to make a rough drawing.

texture the look or feel of something.

Websites

To learn more about First Drawings, visit **booklinks.abdopublishing.com**. These links are routinely monitored and updated to provide the most current information available.

Index